CW00516602

Smoothie Recipe Book:

100 Perfect Smoothies Recipes for Weight Loss Detox, Cleanse and Feel Great in Your Body

Teresa Moore

Your Free Gift

I wanted to show my appreciation that you support my work so I've put together a free gift for you.

Big Diabetic Cookbook:

101 Diabetic Recipes for Living Well with Type 2 Diabetes

Just visit the link above to download it now.

I know you will love this gift.

Thanks!

Table of Contents:

Smoothie of feijoa with spinach

Green smoothies with citrus juice

Mandarin-pineapple smoothies with buckwheat flakes

Grape smoothies with green tea

Smoothies of mango and pear with buckwheat flakes

Smoothies with avocado

Strawberry and cowberry smoothies

Apricot-mango smoothies

Smoothies of pineapple with rhubarb

Smoothies made of pineapple and black currant

Raspberry-pineapple smoothies

Apricot-banana smoothie

Berry smoothies with green tea

Green smoothies with orange juice

Nectar smoothie with Goji berries

Beetroot smoothies

Berry smoothies with "Activia"

Smoothies of pineapple and figs

Smoothies with black chokeberry

Vanilla smoothie from kiwi and melon

Orange smoothies

Autumn berry smoothies

Smoothies berry with muesli

Berry smoothies with cinnamon

Sunny smoothies with honey

Green smoothies with pineapple

Smoothies with apricot and kiwi

Mint grape smoothies

Smoothies with Goji berries

Smoothies of nettles and beets

Fruit cocktail with mint "Tropic"

Smoothies with melon, mango, sorrel and basil

Berry smoothies

Fruit smoothie with avocado

Smoothies with chestnuts and grapefruit

Chocolate smoothie based on oat milk

Smoothies with blueberries and bananas with tea

Green banana smoothie with spinach

Smoothies with oatmeal

Carrot and mango smoothies with physalis

Slushy-pear smoothies

Nourishing banana smoothies for the morning

Smoothies of banana and kiwi on milk

Strawberry-raspberry smoothies

Blueberry smoothies with cream

Tangerine smoothies with sage and feijoa

Smoothies "Spinach with kalpisom"

Smoothies "Rhubarb with Peach"

Banana-Apricot Frozen with Raspberry

Citrus Frozen with Strawberries and Vanilla

Smoothies with melon and strawberries

Smoothies for breakfast

Smoothies

Smoothies of mango and banana

Yoghurt smoothies with kiwi, banana and blueberries

Smoothies of melon and watermelon

Smoothie's kefir and vegetable

Summer smoothies with strawberries

Fruity smoothies with green tea

Banana-mango smoothies

Apricot-mint smoothie

Tangerine smoothie with yogurt

Smoothies of goat's milk with berries and honey

Banana smoothie with cinnamon

Smoothies of apple, banana, pineapple and lemon

Smoothies with orange, banana and pineapple

Introduction

The wellness program is based on diet shakes from green leafy vegetables, fruits and water. These weight loss drinks are nutritious and useful, and also very easy to prepare. Throughout this program, you will eat the foods needed to cleanse the cells and internal organs. Bloating, constipation, indigestion, lack of energy, fatigue, blurred consciousness, depression, overweight, chronic pain, infections, allergies, headaches and bowel problems - all these symptoms indicate an increased content of toxins in the body. Each of these protein shakes for weight loss is a true universal medicine, the healing properties of which are confirmed by dozens of specialists.

Avocado-celery smoothies

Ingredients:

- Avocado 1 piece
- Celery 1 stalk
- Soy sauce 1 teaspoon
- Fresh ginger 1 piece
- Lime juice 1 teaspoon
- Olive oil 1 teaspoon
- Pepper black ground pinch
- Black salt pinch
- Water 50 ml

Preparation:

1. Put the avocado, sliced into pieces, a celery stalk and a couple of small pieces of ginger into the blender.
2. Add olive oil, lime juice, soy sauce or balsamic vinegar.
3. Add a pinch of pepper and salt.
4. A small amount of water and all smaleya in puree consistency and guacamole.

Pineapple-mint smoothie

Ingredients:
- Pineapple ¼ pcs
- Fresh mint 10 stems
- Lime 1 piece
- Oranges 3 pieces

Preparation:
1. For the basis of smoothies squeeze out the juice from oranges and lime.
2. 1/4 of pineapple peels and removes the core, then cut into medium pieces.
3. Cut off mint leaves from the stems.
4. Pineapple, mint leaves and juice of oranges and lime, pour in the blender at high speed for about 5 minutes until complete homogeneity.

Green smoothies with spinach and pears

Ingredients:
- Ginger 100 g
- Apples 2 pieces
- Pears 2 pieces
- Spinach 70 g
- Celery stalk 1 piece
- Lime 1 piece

Preparation:
1. Squeeze the juice out of lime.
2. Squeeze the juice from the apples, celery stalk and peeled ginger root about 1 cm long. If you like more sharply, you can take more ginger.
3. Take soft pears, for this recipe is perfectly suited already softened pears, which have lost their firmness and appearance, but have not turned into mush.
4. Cut the pears into 4 pieces and remove the core.
5. Put all the ingredients in a blender and punch at a maximum speed of about 5 minutes.

The greenest in the world of smoothies

Ingredients:
- Fresh spinach leaves 1 g
- Avocado 1 piece
- Pears 2 pieces
- Apples 3 pieces
- Celery 2 stems
- Green basil
- Lime 1 piece
- Honeydew melon 1 piece

Preparation:
1. Squeeze juice from lime in any accessible way.
2. Peel the avocado and cut it large. Immediately pour lime juice to avoid blackening.
3. Treat the pear according to its softness.
4. If the pear is very ripe and soft, remove the seeds and place together with the avocado in the mixer, cut into medium pieces.
5. If the pear is strong, go to the next step. Squeeze juice from pears, apples and celery.
6. Piece of melon peel and cut into medium pieces.
7. Add all this together with the basil leaves in a blender for 5 minutes until smooth.

Smoky Basil Smoothies

Ingredients:

- Melon 1 kg
- Green basil 1 bunch
- Lime 1 piece
- Oranges 2 pieces

Preparation:

1. A piece of melon or melon whole cut into large pieces, remove the seeds and cut the skin.
2. Then cut the melon into medium pieces so that the blender can grind them.
3. Basil washed if necessary and a large tear.
4. Squeeze the juice for the stem. From lime, in order to balance the sweet melon. From oranges, so smoothies were not very thick.
5. All the ingredients are placed in a blender and pierced to a uniform state for about 5 minutes at maximum speed.
6. Serve with a lime slice.

Mandarin-carrot-pineapple smoothies

Ingredients:
- Pineapple 1 kg
- Mandarins 6 pieces
- Carrot 2 pieces
- Lime ½ piece

Preparation:
1. Clean a piece of pineapple weighing about 1 kg.
2. Peel the carrots and squeeze out the juice.
3. For juice it is better to take tangerines with strong skin, soft to squeeze the juice, if you use Abkhaz or Turkish with soft skin, it is better to increase their number to 8 pieces, as the juice will be less.
4. To balance the sour, squeeze the juice out of 0.5 limes.
5. Place all the ingredients in a blender and punch at maximum speed until smooth.

Green smoothies with spinach and kiwi

Ingredients:

- Kiwi 5 pieces
- Lime ½ pcs
- Apples 2 pieces
- Cucumber 3 pieces
- Young spinach 40g

Preparation:

1. Squeeze the juice from apples and cucumbers.
2. Cut the kiwi into halves and use a spoon to remove the flesh, removing the hard part of the stem.
3. Squeeze the juice from the half lime.
4. Put in the blender apple juice and cucumber, lime juice, kiwi halves and leaves of young spinach.
5. Punch in the blender at maximum speed for 5 minutes.

Cowberry-orange smoothie

Ingredients:

- Fresh frozen cowberry 100 g
- Oranges 1 piece
- Milk 200 ml
- Honey 2 teaspoons
- Nuts 50g

Preparation:

1. Squeeze out the orange juice.
2. Grind the nuts and cranberries in the blender.
3. Add to cowberry-nut mixture milk, orange juice and honey. It is good to shake and pour on glasses.

Strawberry-milk smoothies with basil and feijoa

Ingredients:

- Strawberry 200 g
- Vanilla Ice Cream 100 g
- Milk 200 ml
- Lemon juice 2 teaspoons
- Green basil 1 stem
- Vanilla sugar 5 g
- Feijoa ½ pcs

Preparation:

1. Mix the ingredients in a blender and whisk until smooth.

Inky Smoothies

Ingredients:

- Bilberry 100 g
- Bananas 2 pieces
- Fresh mint
- Apple 1 piece

Preparation:

1. Mix all the ingredients in a blender.
2. You can add apricots.

Smoothies with grapefruit, banana and cranberries

Ingredients:
- Grapefruits ½ pieces
- Bananas 1 piece
- Frozen cranberries 20 g
- Honey

Preparation:
1. Mix in a blender half a grapefruit, banana and cranberries.
2. Melt honey in a microwave until liquid.
3. Add it to the total mixture. Mix.
4. Pour the resulting smoothie into a glass and enjoy.

Smoothies of black currant, banana and nectarine

Ingredients:
- Black currant 2 cups
- Banana 1 piece
- Nectarines 6 pieces
- Oranges 6 pieces

Preparation:
1. Squeeze the juice from the oranges.
2. Remove the twigs from the black currant.
3. Cut the banana large.
4. Remove the nectarines from the bones and cut them large.
5. Put everything in the blender, punch at a maximum speed of about 5 minutes.
6. Then wipe through a sieve to remove currant bones.

Refreshing strawberry smoothies

Ingredients:

- Frozen strawberry 10 pieces
- Lemon 1 piece
- Fresh mint 1 bunch
- Green tea 15 g

Preparation:

1. Put the strawberries in the blender.
2. Cut the lemon in half and squeeze the juice. For those who do not like too sour, you can only give half.
3. Cooled tea with lemon juice is added to the strawberry.
4. Mint rinsed under a stream of water, tear off the leaves and put in a blender.
5. For lovers of sweetening, you can add a spoonful of honey.

Banana smoothies with blueberries

Ingredients:
- Bananas 2 pieces
- Milk 250 ml
- Frozen blueberries 40 g
- Ice cream 30 g
- Curd 20g

Preparation:
1. Cut the banana with rings, put in a blender.
2. Add ice cream, bilberries and whisk.
3. Add the milk and cottage cheese to the resulting mass. Beat until smooth.

Coffee smoothie with chocolate and banana

Ingredients:
- Milk 100 ml
- Instant coffee 1 teaspoon
- Banana 1 piece
- Coconut shavings 1 teaspoon
- Black chocolate 70% 4 pieces
- Hazelnut 15 g
- Ice 8 pieces

Preparation:
1. All the ingredients, except for grated chocolate and ice, fall asleep in the mixer and bring to the state of the foam sour cream.
2. Pour into a glass, throw ice and sprinkle with grated chocolate.

Smoothies with celery, carrots and apple

Ingredients:
- Carrots 1 piece
- Apple 1 piece
- Celery root 3 pieces

Preparation:
1. Carrots and apple clean.
2. All chop and grind in a blender.

Winter smoothies from avocado, banana and kiwi

Ingredients:

- Banana 1 piece
- Kiwi 1 piece
- Avocado ½ pcs
- Water ½ liter

Preparation:

1. Clean the avocado, kiwi and banana.
2. Cut fruit into the blender bowl.
3. Fill with water.
4. Turn on the blender in the "liquefied" or "puree" mode.
5. We are waiting for 1.5 minutes.

Green smoothies with spinach and ginger

Ingredients:
- Apple 1 piece
- Spinach 1 beam
- Cucumbers 1 piece
- Ginger
- Lime 1 piece
- Honey
- Water 1 glass

Preparation:
1. Wash and clean all vegetables and fruits.
2. Cut everything you need and grind in a blender.
3. Add water, squeeze juice from lime and mix.

Smoothies with strawberries, bananas and pineapples

Ingredients:
- Milk 150 ml
- Strawberries 7 pieces
- Banana 1 piece
- Pineapple 120 g

Preparation:
1. Pour the milk into the blender and add the rest of the ingredients. Strawberries and pineapples can also be used frozen.

Smoothies with sprouts of green buckwheat

Ingredients:
- Green buckwheat 70 g
- Banana 1 piece
- Kiwi 1 piece
- Pear 1 piece
- Honey 1 tablespoon
- Freshly squeezed grapefruit juice 150 ml

Preparation:
Soak the buckwheat with drinking water, rinse after 6 hours, and leave to germinate, rinse every 4 hours. After 24 hours sprouts appeared. For smoothies use fruit. Clear them load them into a glass and add water and honey, sprouted green buckwheat. Carefully break it down. Smoothies ready!

Cherry smoothies with yogurt

Ingredients:

- Cherry 165 g
- Yogurt 4 tablespoons
- Milk 1 glass
- Cinnamon
- Oat flakes 3 tablespoons
- Honey 2 tablespoons

Preparation:

1. Cocktail on the basis of milk and honey can be prepared from any berries. In this case - it will be cherries. To the cocktail you can add yogurt and milk, as well as cinnamon - an important component that will give smoothies a special taste.
2. Oat flakes are mixed with milk and put in a microwave for a few minutes. After that, we send to the blender bowl a washed cherry without a stone and yogurt.
3. We also send oat flakes to milk and start whipping. Gradually add honey. Remember that honey cannot be boiled.
4. Cocktails with berries love cinnamon, especially if it's cherry or apples. Add to taste and start whipping until smooth.
5. The resulting cherry cocktail is poured into glasses and sent to the refrigerator. After 30 minutes smoothies can be put on the table.

Smoothies of avocado and bananas

Ingredients:
- Soymilk 1 liter
- Bananas 4 pieces
- Avocado 400g
- Fresh berries

Preparation:
1. Peel and cut bananas with slices, cut the avocado, remove the stone and separate the pulp from the peel.
2. Place all the ingredients for the smoothie in the mixing bowl.
3. Whip in "Blender" mode, speed - 7, time - 30 seconds.
4. Pour the smoothies into glasses, decorate with fresh berries and serve immediately.

Mango-Citrus smoothie

Ingredients:
- Mango 1 piece
- Oranges 2 pieces
- Kiwi 2 pieces
- Stem of celery 4 stems

Preparation:
1. One large mango mine and cut into slices, two oranges and two kiwis are cleaned cut and add to the mango. Fruit the fruit in a bowl and whisk in a blender. We pass through the juicer four stalks of fresh celery. Add to the fruit sauce.

Smoothies of beet and avocado with detox effect

Ingredients:

- Beetroot 1 piece
- Avocado ½ pcs
- Stem of celery 1 stalk
- Strawberry 100 g
- Apple 1 piece
- Lemon juice

Preparation:

1. Take a small beet root. Whip all the ingredients in the blender.

Raspberry smoothies with mint from "Mitten Coffee"

Ingredients:
- Raspberry frozen 80 g
- Apple 80g
- Fresh mint 10 g
- Apple juice without pulp 130 ml

Preparation:
1. We clean the apple and cut slices, put it in a blender. Add the frozen raspberries, mint leaves and apple juice to the apple.

Smoothies with apple and banana

Ingredients:
- Apple 1 piece
- Banana 1 piece
- Honey 1 teaspoon
- Natural low-fat yogurt 2 tablespoons
- Low-fat milk 200 ml
- Cinnamon pinch

Preparation:
1. Put in the blender apple, banana, 1 teaspoon of honey, 2 tablespoons of natural yogurt, 200 ml of milk and a pinch of cinnamon.
2. Beat to homogeneity.
3. Optionally add ice.

Pineapple smoothies with yogurt

Ingredients:
- Canned pineapple slices 1 glass
- Concentrated orange juice 1 glass
- Vanilla yogurt ½ cup
- Water ¼ cup
- Ice 2 pieces

Preparation:
1. In a blender mix the pieces of pineapple, orange concentrate, yogurt, water and ice. Whisk until smooth and serve immediately.

Smoothies with green tea leaves

Ingredients:
- Milk 125 ml
- Natural Yoghurt 125 ml
- Banana ½ pcs
- Green tea 1 teaspoon

Preparation:
1. In a tall glass or a glass, mix the yogurt with the milk.
2. Cut a half of the banana and add to the glass.
3. Top with a teaspoon of green tea crushed.

Morning green smoothies

Ingredients:

- Water 1 glass
- Milk 1 glass
- Berries of Assay 100 g
- Powder of spirulina 100 g
- Cocoa Powder 100 g
- Goji Berries 100 g
- Poppy 100 g

Preparation:

1. Mix all ingredients in a blender. In the end, you should get a dark green mixture.

Smoothies with tarragon and feijoa

Ingredients:
- Feijoa 100 g
- Lemon 1 piece
- Oranges 3 pieces
- Fresh tarragon 4 stems

Preparation:
1. Squeeze juice from oranges and half a lemon.
2. Cut the feijoa into halves.
3. Remove the leaves of tarragon from the stems.
4. Punch in a feijoa blender with the squeezed juice of oranges and lemon and tarragon leaves until smooth and pour into tall glasses.

Pineapple-grapefruit smoothies

Ingredients:
- Pineapple 300 g
- Banana 1 piece
- Red grapefruits 2 pieces
- Lime 1 piece

Preparation:
1. Squeeze the juice from lime and grapefruits.
2. Piece of pineapple and remove the core, cut into medium pieces.
3. Peel the banana and cut into medium pieces.
4. Punch in the blender squeezed juice, pineapple and banana.
5. Serve with a piece of pineapple.

Pineapple smoothies root

Ingredients:
- Pineapple 0.3 piece
- Oranges 3 pieces
- Salad corn 1 bunch
- Lemon ½ pcs

Preparation:
1. Wash the corn salad and remove the rootlets.
2. Squeeze for the basics of smoothies juice from orange and half a lemon.
3. Peel the pineapple and remove the core.
4. Put all the ingredients in a blender and punch at high speed until complete homogeneity.

Beetroot pineapple with mashed potatoes and fennel

Ingredients:

- Beetroot 300 g
- Pineapple 0.3 piece
- Fennel 1 piece
- Lime 1 piece

Preparation:

1. Clean 1/3 of the pineapple and remove the core.
2. Peel the beets and squeeze out the juice from the fennel.
3. Squeeze the juice out of lime.
4. Place all the ingredients in a blender and pour at maximum speed until smooth.

Spicy tomato smoothie with pumpkin seeds

Ingredients:
- Stem of celery 50 g
- Beetroot 1 piece
- Carrots 1 piece
- Tomatoes 2 pieces
- Garlic 2 cloves
- Curry ¼ teaspoon
- Turmeric ¼ teaspoon
- Cumin ¼ teaspoon
- Peeled pumpkin seeds 50g

Preparation:
1. Pure everything in a blender, previously cutting the ingredients into cubes.

Smoothie of feijoa with spinach

Ingredients:

- Feijoa 8 pieces
- Mint of 10 stems
- Young spinach 50g
- Apples 3 pieces
- Pears 1 piece
- Lime 1 piece
- Stem of celery 2 pieces

Preparation:

1. Cut off the stalk and cut into four parts and put in a blender.
2. Add mint leaves and spinach.
3. Squeeze juice from pears, celery, limes and apples in any way you can and add all the juice to the blender.
4. Punch at high speed for about 5 minutes. If you get too thick juice, add more freshly squeezed apple juice.

Green smoothies with citrus juice

Ingredients:
- Oranges 2 pieces
- Grapefruits 1 piece
- Spinach 50 g
- Celery root 2 pieces

Preparation:
1. Squeeze the juice out of oranges and grapefruit.
2. Mix everything in the blender until smooth.

Mandarin-pineapple smoothies with buckwheat flakes

Ingredients:
- Mandarins 400g
- Pineapple 700 g
- Rice drinks 400 ml
- Buckwheat flakes 3 tablespoons

Preparation:
1. Clean the tangerines. These are the only citrus fruits, except very ripe oranges, which can be smoothed in a blender, simply by brushing.
2. Piece of pineapple clean and remove the core. Slice the middle chunks.
3. Take 300 ml of rice drink, buckwheat flakes, mandarin slices and pineapple and punch at high speed in a blender.
4. Allow to stand for about 10-15 minutes, during which time the buckwheat flakes will swell.
5. Add another 100ml of rice beverage and pour in the blender again. If the smoothies are still thick, bring water or a rice drink until you need concentration.

Grape smoothies with green tea

Ingredients:

- Water 125 ml
- Green grapes without stones 250 g
- Pineapple 125 g
- Ice 6 pieces
- Green tea 1 teaspoon

Preparation:

1. Pour the green tea with hot water. Cover and let it brew for 5 minutes. Strain and completely cool.
2. Put in the bowl of the blender all the ingredients: grapes, pineapple slices, tea and ice cubes. Beat until smooth.
3. Pour into a glass and serve immediately.

Smoothies of mango and pear with buckwheat flakes

Ingredients:
- Mango 1 piece
- Lemon 1 piece
- Oranges 3 pieces
- Coconut water 1 glass
- Buckwheat flakes ½ cup
- Pear 1 piece

Preparation:
1. Remove the peel from the mango and remove the stone. Slice the middle chunks.
2. Squeeze the juice from 1 lemon and 3 oranges.
3. Buckwheat flakes soak in juice for 10-15 minutes and then pour into a blender. Since they greatly increase in volume.
4. Depending on what kind of pear you use, do the following: if the pear is very hard, then it is better to squeeze the juice out of it, if it is possible, if soft, then remove the core and coarsely cut and put in a blender along with the mango .
5. Add a glass of coconut water and pour in the blender at maximum speed for about 5 minutes.
6. If the smoothie is very dense, add more coconut water and again pour in the blender to bring to the desired consistency.

Smoothies with avocado

Ingredients:

- Avocado 2 pieces
- Apples 3 pieces
- Pear 1 piece
- Celery 2 stems
- Green pepper 1 piece
- Lime

Preparation:

1. Squeeze the juice from green peppers, apples, pears and celery in your way.
2. Avocado cleanse remove the stone and cut into medium pieces.
3. Put everything in the blender and punch at a maximum speed of 5 minutes.
4. Serve by decorating a slice of cucumber.
5. For those who love more, you can add half or whole lime juice.

Strawberry and cowberry smoothies

Ingredients:
- Freshly frozen cranberries 300 g
- Strawberry 500 g
- Oranges 3 pieces

Preparation:
1. Pre-freeze cranberries beforehand.
2. Squeeze out the juice from 3 oranges in any available way.
3. Remove the stem from the strawberry and cut it in half.
4. Put all ingredients in the blender and punch at top speed.
5. Serve with strawberries.

Apricot-mango smoothies

Ingredients:

- Apricots 8 pieces
- Mango 1 piece
- Freshly squeezed orange juice ½ liter
- Lime 1 piece

Preparation:

1. Squeeze juice from oranges and lime or take the ready-made orange juice without sugar with pulp. If you love more, take 1.5 or 2 limes.
2. Clean the mango and remove the stone, cut into medium pieces.
3. Remove the apricots from the apricots, divide into halves.
4. Put all the ingredients in a blender and punch at a maximum speed of about 5 minutes.
5. Check the consistency - if the smoothie is too thick, dilute with orange juice or water and pour in again.
6. Serve by decorating a branch of tarragon.

Smoothies of pineapple with rhubarb

Ingredients:
- Pineapple 0.3 pieces
- Banana 1 piece
- Freshly squeezed orange juice 1 glass
- Rhubarb 2 stems
- Fresh mint

Preparation:
1. Squeeze juice from oranges or take ready juice with pulp.
2. Pineapple and remove the core.
3. At the rhubarb stems, remove the hard end and cut it coarsely.
4. Clean the banana and cut medium.
5. In a blender, pour all the ingredients for about 5 minutes at top speed.
6. If you need to change the consistency, add the juice and try again.
7. Serve with mint leaves.

Smoothies made of pineapple and black currant

Ingredients:

- Pineapple ½ pcs
- Black currant 300 g
- Mint 1 beam
- Soy Milk 2 cups
- Syrup of Agave

Preparation:

1. If you use not fresh, but frozen blackcurrant, then you can either unfreeze it during the night on the top shelf of the refrigerator, or put it in a frozen form, then the smoothie will be cold, but not less tasty.
2. Peel half a pineapple, remove the core and cut into medium pieces.
3. Leave peppermint leaves from the stems, set aside the tops for decoration.
4. In the blender, put sliced pineapple, black currant, mint leaves and pour in soy milk.
5. Punch in the blender at maximum speed for 5 minutes.
6. Try a teaspoon if the pineapple is not very sweet, then the smoothies can turn out to be quite sour, at the expense of currants, then add to the taste 1 or 2 tablespoons of agave syrup or light honey and punch again.
7. Serve with mint leaves.

Raspberry-pineapple smoothies

Ingredients:
- Raspberry 500 g
- Pineapple ½ pcs
- Fresh mint 4 stems
- Rice vanilla milk 1 glass

Preparation:
1. Pineapple is cleaned, remove the core and cut into 4 parts along and then in thin slices.
2. In a blender, pour raspberries, pineapple, rice milk and mint leaves. If there is time and desire, you can punch raspberries in a blender separately and wipe through a sieve getting rid of pits.
3. Punch about 5 minutes at top speed.
4. Check the density and if necessary add more rice milk and punch again.
5. Pour into the glasses decorating the top leaves of fresh mint.

Apricot-banana smoothie

Ingredients:
- Apricots 12 pieces
- Banana 1 piece
- Rice Vanilla Milk 250 ml
- Natural yoghurt 125 ml

Preparation:
1. Remove the apricots from the apricots and pour in with the banana and rice milk, yogurt and banana in the blender at a maximum speed of about 5 minutes.
2. Serve, decorated with young leaves of mint and a piece of apricot.

Berry smoothies with green tea

Ingredients:

- Frozen cranberries ½ cup
- Frozen blueberries0 cups
- Frozen blackberry ¼ cup
- Strawberry 5 pieces
- Banana 1 piece
- Soy Milk ¼ cup
- Green tea ½ cup
- Honey 2 tablespoons
- Cane sugar

Preparation:

1. Mix berries in a blender, add green tea, soy milk and honey.
2. Mix well, add sugar to taste and pour berry smoothies with green tea into glasses.

Green smoothies with orange juice

Ingredients:

- Carrots 1 piece
- Broccoli cabbage 4 heads
- Spinach 75 g
- Apple 1 piece
- Orange juice 250 ml

Preparation:

1. Mix everything in a blender, add orange juice.
2. Stir well, and pour smoothies into glasses.

Nectar smoothie with Goji berries

Ingredients:
- Nectarines 4 pieces
- Oranges 3 pieces
- Red grapefruits 1 piece
- Lime 1 piece
- Berry Goji 2 tablespoons

Preparation:
1. Squeeze juice from oranges and grapefruit and lime.
2. Peaches cut into medium pieces.
3. Break through the blender peaches, citrus juice and goji berries.
4. Serve with a piece of nectarine.

Beetroot smoothies

Ingredients:

- Beetroot 1 piece
- Kiwi 2 pieces
- Apple ½ g
- Plums 1 g

Preparation:

1. Peel the beets and kiwi from the peel.
2. Peeled beets and kiwi cut into small pieces. Then cut the apple and the sink.
3. All ingredients should be placed in a blender and mixed at medium speed.
4. If the smoothies seem too thick, get some water.

Berry smoothies with "Activia"

Ingredients:

- Banana 2 pieces
- "Activia natural" 1 glass
- Frozen strawberry 8 pieces
- Green grapes pitted 50g
- Black currant ½ cup

Preparation:

1. Add berries and fruits to the blender.
2. Pour the yogurt.
3. Mix in a blender for 3-4 minutes.

Smoothies of pineapple and figs

Ingredients:
- Pineapple ½ pcs
- Carrots 4 pieces
- Figs 2 pieces
- Oranges 5 pieces
- Lemon 1 piece

Preparation:
1. For a basis to squeeze juice from carrots and squeeze out juice from oranges and a lemon.
2. Peel and remove the pineapple, cut into medium pieces.
3. In the blender we break through the chopped figs, pineapple, and orange and carrot juice.
4. If necessary, the density is regulated by adding water or juice.
5. Serve with a piece of fresh carrots.

Smoothies with black chokeberry

Ingredients:
- Chokeberry 1 cup
- Banana 1 piece
- Apples 4 pieces
- Lemon 1 piece
- Carrot 3 pieces
- Avocado 1 piece

Preparation:
1. Squeeze juice from 4 large green apples and carrots.
2. Chokeberry removes from the branches and well mine.
3. Squeeze the juice from the lemon.
4. Avocado clean and remove the stone.
5. In the blender we break through the avocado, banana, chokeberry, apple-carrot juice and a glass of milk for 5 minutes until homogeneity.
6. If necessary, add more juice or milk in order to achieve the desired consistency and break through again.
7. Serve it with a piece of apple.

Vanilla smoothie from kiwi and melon

Ingredients:
- Kiwi 4 pieces
- Melon 3 pieces
- Mint ½ beam
- Lemon 1 piece
- Soy vanilla milk 500 ml

Preparation:
1. Kiwi should be cleaned and put the flesh in a blender.
2. Cut 3 pieces of melon into medium pieces.
3. Squeeze the juice from 1 lemon.
4. There also add mint leaves, soy vanilla milk, 0.5 lemon juice.
5. Punch at top speed for 5 minutes. Try and add more lemon juice, if your taste is very sweet.

Orange smoothies

Ingredients:

- Banana 2 pieces
- Pineapple ½ pcs
- Carrots 4 pieces
- Avocado 1 piece
- Lemon 1 piece

Preparation:

1. Two bananas half a peeled pineapple with a remote core pours freshly squeezed carrot juice.
2. Put everything in the blender; add the avocado, which will give the silky smoothies, juice of half a lemon and attention to the key ingredient.
3. Tablespoon of powder lukuma.
4. Punch all at maximum speed for 5 minutes and serve.

Autumn berry smoothies

Ingredients:

- Chokeberry 1 cup
- Fresh cranberries 1 glass
- Cowberry 1 glass
- Banana 1 piece
- Avocado 1 piece

Preparation:

1. In a blender, put a glass of cranberries, a glass of black cherry, a glass of cowberry, and a large banana.
2. To obtain a softer flavor, add one ripe avocado and 400 ml of rice milk.
3. We punch well at maximum speed until complete homogeneity.

Smoothies berry with muesli

Ingredients:

- Strawberries 7 pieces
- Bilberry 100 g
- Muesli 2 tablespoons
- Milk 1 glass
- Dried fruits 1 tablespoon

Preparation:

1. Mix all the ingredients in the blender; add the milk, although you can replace it with any liquid yogurt or kefir.
2. Ask the program for smoothies and, after a few minutes, pour into glasses.

Berry smoothies with cinnamon

Ingredients:
- Bilberry 100 g
- Banana 1 piece
- Cherry juice ½ cup
- Cinnamon ½ teaspoon
- Lemon juice 1 teaspoon

Preparation:
1. Banana cut into slices, add blueberries, half a cup of cherry juice, squeeze out a slice of lemon and a half-spoonful of cinnamon.
2. All the ingredients are loaded into the blender and mix for 1-2 minutes. Ready smoothies to decorate with blueberries and a slice of lemon!

Sunny smoothies with honey

Ingredients:

- Grapefruits 1 piece
- Peach 1 piece
- Pineapple ½ pcs
- Carrot juice ½ cup
- Honey 1 teaspoon

Preparation:

1. Pineapple chopped, grapefruit and peach peeled and cut into slices.
2. Sliced pineapple, peach, grapefruit and pour carrot juice and add honey. Mix all the ingredients in a blender for 3-5 minutes.
3. Ready to smooth the smoothie with a slice of peach.

Green smoothies with pineapple

Ingredients:

- Kiwi 2 pieces
- Spinach 3 Beams
- Pineapple ½ piece

Preparation:

1. Kiwi cleaned, cut into cubes, and cut into pineapple.
2. Add kiwi, pineapple, spinach to the blender. Stir for 2-3 minutes before the appearance of airy foam.

Smoothies with apricot and kiwi

Ingredients:
- Apricots 5 pieces
- Kiwi 2 pieces
- Cherry 9 pieces
- Apple juice 1 glass

Preparation:
1. Clear the kiwi fruit.
2. Cut kiwi and apricots into slices.
3. Put everything in a blender, pour juice and whip.

Mint grape smoothies

Ingredients:
- Red grapes 150 g
- Frozen cherry 100 g
- Fresh mint 100 g
- Dates 2 pieces
- Water 150 ml

Preparation:
1. Use more dates if the grapes are not sweet
2. You cannot put dates if the grapes are very sweet
3. If your blender does not cope with mint leaves or you did not find them, then you can use water instead of water, in which the dry mint was pre-baked, do not forget to cool the water.

Smoothies with Goji berries

Ingredients:

- Bananas 6 pieces
- Goji Berries 3 tablespoons
- Frozen strawberry 200 g

Preparation:

1. Load the ingredients into a blender and mix until smooth.
2. Pour the smoothies over the glasses; decorate with pieces of banana and Goji berries.

Smoothies of nettles and beets

Ingredients:
- Young Nettles 2 Beams
- Beetroot 1 piece
- Banana 1 piece
- Water 500 ml

Preparation:
1. Beet and banana to clean grind in a blender with nettle and water.

Fruit cocktail with mint "Tropic"

Ingredients:

- Pears 500 g
- Oranges 800 g
- Kiwi 300 g
- Fresh mint

Preparation:

1. Peel and slice the fruit.
2. Place all the ingredients for the cocktail in the mixing bowl.
3. Whip in "Blender" mode, speed - 7, time - 30 seconds.
4. Pour the cocktails into glasses, decorate with mint sprigs and serve immediately.

Smoothies with melon, mango, sorrel and basil

Ingredients:
- Melon 1 piece
- Mango ½ pcs
- Oranges 4 pieces
- Sorrel ½ beam
- Syrup Agave 2 tablespoons
- Flower pollen 1 tablespoon

Preparation:
1. Mango is cleaned and cut with a knife pieces of medium size, such that the blender is ground.
2. Cut a piece of melon into the middle pieces and throw it into the blender
3. There, too, rinsed sorrel and basil together with stems
4. We put a spoonful of bee pollen.
5. Squeeze out the juice from 4 oranges
6. Pour into the blender there; too, a little agave syrup can be replaced with maple syrup
7. All this is punched at a high speed for about 5 minutes and served with a mint leaf.

Berry smoothies

Ingredients:
- Cherry pitted 100g
- Banana 1 piece
- Apple 1 piece
- Almond 100 g
- Mint leaves pinch
- Sweet Cherry 100g

Preparation:
1. Whisk cherries, cherries, banana, and apple. Add almonds and mint leaves.
2. In these fruits and berries a lot of melatonin, which will help if you cannot sleep.

Fruit smoothie with avocado

Ingredients:

- Apricots 100g
- Apple 1 piece
- Strawberry 100 g
- Figs 100 g
- Avocado 1 piece
- Mango 1 piece

Preparation:

1. Here you need aphrodisiacs: prepare a mixture of apricots, apples, strawberries, figs, avocados and mangoes.

Smoothies with chestnuts and grapefruit

Ingredients:

- Egg yolk 40 g
- Sugar 20g
- Milk 250 ml
- Grapefruit juice 100 ml
- Gelatin in plates of 1,5 pieces
- Grapefruits 2 pieces
- White small sugar 50 g
- Chestnut purees 200 g

Preparation:

1. On the eve of mixing in a bowl of egg yolks with sugar. Pour 100 ml of hot milk, stir and pour the mixture into a saucepan. Cook over low heat until the mixture sticks to the spoon. After the end of cooking, pour into silicone molds in the form of ice cubes and put it in the freezer for the night.

2. The next day, drain the grapefruit juice through a sieve. 1/4 of the juice should be heated. Plate gelatin for 5 minutes soak in cold water, squeeze and mix with hot juice. Stir well, add cold juice. To spill on glasses. Put it in the fridge for 2 hours to keep the jelly.

3. Remove the zest from the grapefruits and squeeze the juice out of them. Blanch zest: boil it for 10 seconds and remove from water. Repeat this operation twice, each time changing the water. Then put the zest into a bowl of cold water. Allow to drain water. Stir the peel with a little sugar and squeezed juice and cook for 30 minutes on low heat. Beat with a mixer. Let cool and pour over jelly glasses. Put in the fridge while you are preparing smoothies.

4. Pour a chestnut cream, milk and ice cream into the mixer bowl from an English cream. Beat and pour into glasses.

Chocolate smoothie based on oat milk

Ingredients:

- Bananas 2 pieces
- Oatmeal 400 ml
- Powder of carob fruits 1 tablespoon
- Water ½ cup
- Coconut shaving 2 tablespoons
- Dates without pits 4 pieces
- Ground cinnamon ½ teaspoon
- Vanilla pods 1 piece

Preparation:

1. Clear bananas.
2. Fold all the ingredients in a blender
3. Beat well and enjoy!

Smoothies with blueberries and bananas with tea

Ingredients:
- Oranges 4 pieces
- Banana 1 piece
- Coconut oil 1 tablespoon
- Chia seeds 1 tablespoon
- Frozen blueberries 4 tablespoons
- Match Tea pinch
- Rice bran pinch

Preparation:
1. Squeeze juice from oranges
2. Punch in a blender with coconut oil, frozen blueberries and a banana
3. Pour into a glass and decorate from above.

Green banana smoothie with spinach

Ingredients:

- Banana 1 piece
- Fresh spinach leaves 1 bunch
- Lemon juice 1 tablespoon
- Pineapple 1 piece
- Natural low fat yogurt ½ cup
- Water ½ cup
- Grated ginger pinch

Preparation:

1. Fold all the ingredients in a blender and beat.
2. If the cocktail is too thick, add a little more water.

Smoothies with oatmeal

Ingredients:

- Banana 1 piece
- Apple 1 piece
- Almonds 1 teaspoon
- Oat flakes ¼ cup
- Water ¼ cup
- Low-fat milk ½ cup
- Natural low-fat yogurt 2 tablespoons
- Cinnamon pinch
- Honey ½ teaspoon
- Ice to taste

Preparation:

1. Cut an apple.
2. Pour oat flakes with water and put in microwave for 2 minutes.
3. Fold all the remaining ingredients in a blender and mix until smooth.
4. Add the oatmeal and whisk again.
5. If you want, sprinkle the smoothies on top of the almonds.

Carrot and mango smoothies with physalis

Ingredients:
- Mango 100 g
- Carrots 85 g
- Physalis 50 g
- Orange juice 125 ml
- Ground cinnamon pinch
- Orange jam ½ teaspoon

Preparation:
1. Mango clean, separate the flesh from the bones and cut into large pieces. Carrots clean and grate on medium grater. Physalis clean, wash and dry.
2. Prepared ingredients mixed with orange juice and cinnamon in a blender. Try it, add orange jam and mix again.
3. Ready smoothies to pour on glasses, decorate with orange slices and immediately serve.

Slushy-pear smoothies

Ingredients:
Water 250 ml
Garam Masala 2 pieces
Plums 200g
Pears 1 piece
Grape juice 500 ml
Lemon juice 15 ml
Muesli 60 g
Yoghurt 125 g

Preparation:
1. Boil water and pour the tea bags with masala. Infuse for 10 minutes.
2. Pears and plums wash and remove pits. Mix all the ingredients in a blender.
3. Ready smoothies to pour on glasses and decorate with a lemon slice.

Nourishing banana smoothies for the morning

Ingredients:
Milk 1 glass
Banana 1,5 pieces
Oatmeal 5 tablespoons
Ground cinnamon 1 teaspoon
Vanilla on the tip of the knife
Honey 1 teaspoon

Preparation:
1. In the blender, grind oatmeal.
2. Remove peel from bananas and grind too.
3. Add the milk. Beat.
4. Put the rest of the ingredients: cinnamon, honey, vanilla. Beat.

Smoothies of banana and kiwi on milk

Ingredients:
Banana 1 piece
Kiwi 1 piece
Honey 1 tablespoon
Milk 200 ml

Preparation:
1. Banana to break into pieces and put in a blender.
2. Then cut the peeled kiwi.
3. Add a spoonful of honey and milk.
4. Beat all the ingredients in the blender until smooth, pour into glasses and decorate with a slice of banana or kiwi. Your energy drink is ready.

Strawberry-raspberry smoothies

Ingredients:
Bananas 2 pieces
Raspberry frozen 3 tablespoons
Strawberry yogurt ½ cans
Strawberry purees ½ cans

Preparation:
1. Mix in a blender raspberry, yogurt, mashed potatoes and 1 banana.
2. Pour into a beautiful glass.
3. Cut the banana into pieces, and put it on top.
4. You can decorate with strawberries or raspberries.

Blueberry smoothies with cream

Ingredients:
Frozen blueberries 1 tablespoon
Banana
Strawberries 2 pieces
Cream 2.5 ml
Oatmeal 5 g

Preparation:
1. Place the fruit and rump in the blender.
2. Beat.
3. Put in a glass.
4. Add the cream.

Tangerine smoothies with sage and feijoa

Ingredients:
Mandarins 150g
Sage leaves 1 g
Feijoa 70 g
Ice 70 g
Water 50 ml
Honey 40g

Preparation:
1. Mix all the ingredients in a blender;
2. Pour the contents of the blender into a glass.

Smoothies "Spinach with kalpisom"

Ingredients:
Calpis 25 ml
Coconut milk 230 ml
Spinach 40 g
Sugar syrup 25 ml

Preparation:
1. Combine all the ingredients and punch in a blender.
2. Pour into a glass.

Smoothies "Rhubarb with Peach"

Ingredients:
Rhubarb 120 g
Peach juice 100 ml
Caramel syrup 25 ml
Lemon juice 20 ml
Dried apricots 50g

Preparation:
1. Put all the ingredients in the blender and punch.
2. Pour into a glass.
3. Decorate with dried apricots on a skewer.

Banana-Apricot Frozen with Raspberry

Ingredients:
Banana 80 g
Apricot jams 30 g
Lemon juice 40 ml
Ice 180 g
Raspberries puree 40 g

Preparation:
1. Place all ingredients except raspberries in a blender, beaten.
2. Put raspberry puree on the bottom layer in a jar, then use a bar spoon to lay the contents of the blender with the top layer.

Citrus Frozen with Strawberries and Vanilla

Ingredients:
Lemon juice 50 ml
Lemon 10 g
Vanilla syrup 20 ml
Sugar syrup 20 ml
Ice 200 g
Strawberry purees 40 g

Preparation:
1. Put all the ingredients except the strawberry puree in a blender, beaten.
2. Using a bar spoon; shift the contents of the blender into the jar.
3. Top with strawberry puree.

Smoothies with melon and strawberries

Ingredients:
Melon 250 g
Frozen strawberry 1 glass
Biscuit
Vanilla milk 3 tablespoons

Preparation:
Throw all ingredients in a blender or mixer and mix.

Smoothies for breakfast

Ingredients:
Oat flakes ½ cup
Milk 1 glass
Blackberry 120 g
Natural yogurt 2 tablespoons
Banana 1 piece
Honey to taste
Ice to taste

Preparation:
1. Scroll in the blender oat flakes, milk, banana, berries and yogurt.
2. If not sweet enough, add honey and beat again.
3. Spill on glasses, put ice and serve.

Smoothies

Ingredients:
Banana 1 piece
Grapefruits ½ piece
Apple ½ piece
Oranges 2 pieces

Preparation:
1. Banana and half the apple turn into a mash.
2. Squeeze out the juice from 2 oranges and half a grapefruit.
3. Stir in the blender.

Smoothies of mango and banana

Ingredients:
Banana 1 piece
Mango 1 piece
Freshly squeezed orange juice 500 ml
Natural yoghurt 4 tablespoons

Preparation:
1. Cut the mango in half and pull out the stone. Cut into strips and throw into the blender. Peel and cut the banana, add to the mango. Add the juice.
2. Mix everything in a blender until smooth. Pour into glasses and add ice.

Yoghurt smoothies with kiwi, banana and blueberries

Ingredients:
Bananas 5 pieces
Bilberry 250 g
Drinking yoghurt 500 ml
Kiwi 5 pieces

Preparation:
1. Bananas, kiwi, blueberries mix and grind with a blender.
2. Add yogurt to this mass.

Smoothies of melon and watermelon

Ingredients:
Honeydew melon 1 piece
Cantaloupe 1 piece
Watermelon 400 g
Lemonade "Citro" ½ cup
Crushed ice ½ cup

Preparation:
1. Put in the blender chopped melon, cantaloupe and watermelon, add crushed ice and pour the sieve.
2. Beat to a homogeneous mass.
3. Pour into glasses and serve.

Smoothie's kefir and vegetable

Ingredients:
Tomato 1 piece
Garlic 2 cloves
Vegetable oil
Beetroot 1 piece
Carrot 1 piece
Greenery
Cucumber 2 pieces

Preparation:
1. Peel the beets and carrots.
2. Carrots, beets, cucumbers should be crushed in a blender chopper, or grated on a large grater.
3. Greens or grind in a chopper, or chop less.
4. Cut the tomatoes in smaller, cubes.
5. Grind the garlic in a crust.
6. Shredded vegetables put in a deep bowl, add salt, pepper, other condiments to taste, vegetable oil. You can add something else: grated zucchini, sweet pepper - any vegetable set, like anyone likes. You can soy sauce, if you want.
7. Stir like an ordinary green salad. This is the basis. It can be transferred to a jar and stored in a refrigerator.
8. To prepare 1-2 servings put in a blender about 4 tablespoons vegetable salad and pour kefir so that it only covers the vegetables.
9. Grind in a blender to a homogeneous mass, the vegetables should be like very small sawdust, so that you can drink.
10. If you want to, add kefir.

Summer smoothies with strawberries

Ingredients:
Strawberry 100 g
Kefir 150 ml
Lemon juice 1 teaspoon
Ice
Sugar powder 2 tablespoons

Preparation:
1. Wash strawberries and dry them. Mix with the rest of the ingredients. Optionally add a couple of ice cubes.
2. Beat in a mixer until smooth. Pour into a glass.

Fruity smoothies with green tea

Ingredients:
Peaches 1 piece
Green grapes 100 g
Melon ½ pcs
Honey 3 tablespoons
Freshly brewed green tea ¾ cups
Lemon juice 1 tablespoon

Preparation:
1. Cut the peaches and peeled melon into small pieces and freeze together with the grapes.
2. In the blender, mix frozen fruit, lightly cooled tea, honey and lemon juice. Whisk until smooth and serve immediately.

Banana-mango smoothies

Ingredients:
Mango 1 piece
Banana 1 piece
Natural Yoghurt 300 g

Preparation:
1. Grind the mango and banana well in a blender.
2. Add the yogurt. Mix.

Apricot-mint smoothie

Ingredients:
Apricots 5 pieces
Kefir 1% ½ l
Fresh mint 2 stems
Transparent honey 20 ml

Preparation:
1. Remove the stone from the apricots, and cut the flesh into large pieces.
2. Separate the mint leaves from the stem, chop half the leaves, and leave half for the decor.
3. Add apricots, crushed mint, kefir and honey to the blender bowl.
4. Blend well with a blender until smooth.

Tangerine smoothie with yogurt

Ingredients:
Bananas 2 pieces
Tangerines 3 pieces
Yoghurt 300 g

Preparation:
1.   Cut the bananas. Mix the ingredients. Beat in a blender.

Smoothies of goat's milk with berries and honey

Ingredients:
Necklace milk 1 glass
Frozen strawberries
Frozen blueberries
Banana 1 piece
Honey
Crushed ice

Preparation:
1. Mix frozen berries, milk and ice. Beat in a blender until smooth. Add the banana, honey and whisk again.

Banana smoothie with cinnamon

Ingredients:
Banana 2 pieces
Milk 1.5 cups
Ground cinnamon ¼ teaspoon
Natural low-fat yogurt 1 cup
Ground nutmeg
Mint

Preparation:
1. Peel the bananas, chop and refrigerate in the freezer.
2. Whisk the bananas in the blender. Milk, nutmeg and cinnamon until a homogeneous mass is formed.
3. Pour over the glasses and, if desired, decorate with mint.

Smoothies of apple, banana, pineapple and lemon

Ingredients:
Lemon 1 piece
Apple 1 piece
Banana 1 piece
Pineapple ¼ pcs

Preparation:
1. Cut the apple into slices and pass through the juicer.
2. Turn the resulting apple juice into a blender with lemon juice and a banana.
3. Remove the rind from the pineapple and cut the flesh.
4. Put in a blender and whisk until smooth.
5. Serve with ice or whip with 4-5 ice cubes.

Smoothies with orange, banana and pineapple

Ingredients:
Pineapple 1 piece
Freshly squeezed orange juice ½ cup
Banana 1 piece
Lime 1 piece

Preparation:
1. Peel the pineapple and remove the core. Half of the pineapple is passed through the juicer. Cut the second half into slices and send to a blender, add orange juice, pineapple juice and a banana.
2. Squeeze the lime juice and whisk until smooth.

Printed in Great Britain
by Amazon